A CELEBRATION OF THE 1985 ST. LOUIS CARDINALS

Racin' REDBIRDS!

A CELEBRATION OF THE 1985 ST. LOUIS CARDINALS

Racin' REDBIRDS!

BY UNITED PRESS INTERNATIONAL

CONTEMPORARY
BOOKS, INC.
CHICAGO

All photos courtesy of United Press International, Inc.

Copyright © 1985 by United Press International, Inc.
All rights reserved
Published by Contemporary Books, Inc.
180 North Michigan Avenue, Chicago, Illinois 60601
Manufactured in the United States of America
International Standard Book Number: 0-8092-5059-4

Published simultaneously in Canada by Beaverbooks, Ltd.
195 Allstate Parkway, Valleywood Business Park
Markham, Ontario L3R 4T8 Canada

To Cardinal fans everywhere
This book's for you

CONTENTS

FOREWORD

When you put on the uniform of the St. Louis Cardinals, you know about the hard-nosed players of the past, guys who did anything to win. We never let up. We are agents of action, rather than players who are affected by action. That's our style.

What these Cardinals have done is what all the great St. Louis clubs have done throughout history.

In 1982, Lonnie Smith did what Vince Coleman is doing this year. He ran with reckless abandon, he was going on every pitch.

That's the history of the Cardinals. I was that kind of guy, and Enos Slaughter was before me, and Pepper Martin before that. The team has always had somebody up front who could set the table and force the others to eat.

We feel the game of baseball is played on a battlefield and we are foot soldiers. In 1985, guys like Coleman, Willie McGee, Terry Pendleton, and Tommy Herr have proved they will get a run any way they can. That's Cardinal baseball.

Coleman has really sparked the team. I don't think you can steal bases with just speed. You can put all the track stars with all their world-class speed and they couldn't steal bases. You need more; you need passion built on knowledge. You need

that base runner's arrogance. Coleman has that. He does it because he loves to.

There is no defense against speed, unless you want to alter the rules. It throws off the whole fabric of the game.

Speed is great but sometimes you've got to have the power to knock 'em in. Jack Clark and Darrell Porter have been making that kind of contact. Power can win a ball game and the Cardinals have gotten it from these guys.

The pitching staff is the surprising area. The Cardinals have pitchers who have all reached their potential in the same year.

Look at John Tudor, Danny Cox, Kurt Kepshire, Ken Dayley, Jeff Lahti—no one expected them to do so well. Joaquin Andujar, you knew he'd be great. But the others looked like .500 pitchers. I think the last club to put it all together like this was the '69 Mets.

No matter how this season turns out, this club has shown they will pounce on anything once you give them a break. They see an opportunity and they capitalize on it. They get a fuse and they light it.

Just like all the great Cardinal teams of the past.

Lou Brock
Former Cardinal,
Member, Baseball Hall of Fame

1
"WE WON'T FINISH LAST"

Branch Wesley Rickey, born in 1881, grew up to be a major-league ball player, although his .239 lifetime average made him no threat to Ty Cobb. What Rickey lacked in batting skill, he made up for in brains. Today he is revered as the greatest theoretician and talent evaluator baseball has ever known.

When the legendary Rickey died in 1965, Ozzie Smith was 10 years old, Tom Herr was 9, Willie McGee 7, Terry Pendleton 5, and Vince Coleman and Andy Van Slyke 4. Dorrel Norman Elvert Herzog, better known in his profession as Whitey, was 34. Two·years earlier, he had ended a mediocre major-league playing career and was now making a transition from the field to the front office.

On the surface, little connected the above factors to anything that would happen in Busch Stadium one generation later. And yet, Rickey remains a significant factor in the St. Louis Cardinals' 1985 success.

It was Rickey who, among his many other musings, stated years ago that speed was the most important baseball talent because it is the only one that can be used on both offense and defense. Many years later, when building the Cardinals, Herzog followed the same formula.

Herzog, who joined the St. Louis organization in 1980, took one look at Busch Stadium, and decided that quick feet would help him much more than large biceps. After all, the distance was 330 feet from home plate to the corners, 383 to the alleys, and 414 to center. The fence was more than 10 feet tall. A team could grow very lean awaiting for a fat pitch.

Furthermore, Busch Stadium utilized an artificial surface, and Herzog knew all about that. He had just spent five seasons with the Kansas City Royals, generating division championships in the same kind of ballpark. On such a surface, the ball moves quickly—just the right speed for anyone able to adapt.

On offense, the plan was simple: use the whole field. Sneak the base hit between the outfielders. Turn the single into a double, the double into a triple. Steal a base.

On defense, things were just as uncomplicated. Keep the ball in the ballpark. Run down the ball in the outfield. Throw strikes. Let them hit it, and we'll catch it.

From this theory came the spectacle that developed near the banks of the Mississippi in 1985—Vince Coleman stealing his way into the record books—Ozzie Smith playing shortstop the way no one else ever has—Willie McGee collecting seven hits in a double-header—Joaquin Andujar and Danny Cox throwing sizzling strikes—Tom

This would be the year that Ozzie Smith would become the most valuable shortstop in the history of the game . . .

... the year that rookie Vince Coleman would race his way into the record books ...

. . . the year that Jack
Clark would come to roost
with the Cardinals . . .

. . . the year that Joaquin Andujar would win more than 20 games . . .

... the year that Tommy Herr would come from behind in the All-Star voting to beat out 1984 MVP Ryne Sandberg ...

It was throwback baseball. More than 50 years earlier, in 1934, another Cardinal team had played the same way. Pepper Martin stole 23 bases and hit .289. Frankie Frisch hit .305 with 11 steals. Rip Collins hit 35 out of the park. Joe Medwick added 18. Dizzy Dean won 30. The "Gas House Gang" won it all.

Now, things are different. Instead of Sportsman's Park, the site is Busch Stadium. The ace right-hander comes from the Dominican Republic instead of from Arkansas. Players wear double-knits instead of flannels.

Only the cheers are the same. Thanks to Branch Rickey and Whitey Herzog, the Cardinals were playing winning baseball. Before it was over, they would find themselves in a beauty of a pennant race.

Whitey Herzog became the Cardinal manager on June 9, 1980, replacing Ken Boyer. The club had finished third the previous year, had not won a pennant since 1968, and had not captured a World Series since 1967.

The lineup inherited by Herzog consisted of: Keith Hernandez at first base, Ken Oberkfell at second, Garry Templeton at short, Ken Reitz at third, George Hendrick in right field, Tony Scott in center, Leon Durham in left, and Ted Simmons behind the plate.

Forming the pitching staff were Pete Vuckovich, Bob Forsch, Jim Kaat, Bob Sykes, and Silvio Martinez.

Herzog observed his new team for the rest of the season, while the Cardinals finished fourth. Then Herzog began to work. He kept the best players and used the others to acquire what he needed.

The shake-up began in December of 1980, and, in a five-day span, Herzog dealt away 13 players. On December 8, he sent catchers Terry Kennedy and Steve Swisher, infielder Mike Phillips, and pitchers John Littlefield, John Urrea, Kim

. . . and the year that Willie McGee would collect seven hits in a doubleheader.

Herr turns the double play as Ron Cey is out at second; it's Ozzie-to-Tommy-to-Jack.

(Above) **Third baseman Art Howe dives for—and misses—Gary Carter's 11th inning hit.**
(Below) **Giant Gary Rajsich bowls over catcher Tom Nieto.**

The Cards sent Leon Durham to the Cubs for ace reliever Bruce Sutter. Sutter is long gone to the Braves, but Durham's still pounding out hits for the Cubs.

Seaman, and Al Olmstead to San Diego for reliever Rollie Fingers, pitcher Bob Shirley, catcher Gene Tenace, and minor-league catcher Bob Geren.

The next day, he sent outfielder Leon Durham and infielders Ken Reitz and Ty Waller to the Chicago Cubs for relief ace Bruce Sutter.

Finally, on December 12, came the big one, the trade that broke some hearts in St. Louis. Herzog sent Vuckovich, Fingers, and Simmons to Milwaukee for outfielders Sixto Lezcano and David Green, and pitchers Lary Sorensen and Dave LaPoint.

QUESTIONABLE TRADES

In retrospect, the trades appear uneven. Of the players acquired, none remain with the Cardinals. Of the players traded away, Kennedy and Durham are top-talent big leaguers, and Vuckovich, Fingers, and Simmons are still effective pitchers.

But all you can say about the trades is that they improved the team.

"It makes me mad when people ask what this guy's doing or that guy's doing," Herzog said in evaluating his trades. "The bottom line is how is the club doing?"

Herzog continued to deal. He reached back into the Kansas City family and signed catcher Darrell Porter through the reentry draft. He landed Joaquin Andujar from Houston, Willie McGee from the New York Yankees, and Ozzie Smith from San Diego.

After finishing without reward in 1981, when they posted the best overall record in the National League East but neglected to win either half of the split season, the Cardinals emerged in 1982 ready to play ball.

How ready? They won the division by three games, swept Atlanta 3–0 in the playoffs, and beat the Milwaukee Brewers in a seven-game World Series.

REGENERATION

When the Cards came into spring training in 1985, the picture was puzzling. The team was different—much different—from that 1982 Championship team. The 1983 and 1984 seasons had been disappointing. Gone were Keith Hernandez, George Hendrick, and Ken Oberkfell. Even the front office had changed. Fred Kuhlmann became the club's executive vice-president and chief operating officer on November 5, 1984. In the general manager's chair was Dal Maxvill, who was replacing Joe McDonald. Despite Herzog's history of success, some questions existed over who was in charge of the baseball operation.

Even after the World Series triumph, Herzog had continued to trade vigorously. In a deal that proved even less popular than the Ted Simmons trade, Hernandez was dispatched to the New York Mets on June 15, 1983, for pitchers Neil Allen and Rick Ownbey. Oberkfell departed for Atlanta on June 15, 1984, for pitcher Ken

Coleman is off and running—he'll stretch this base hit into a double.

Dayley and utility man Mike Jorgensen. Hendrick went to Pittsburgh on December 12, 1984, as part of a deal that yielded left-hander John Tudor.

With all the shuffling on and off the field, one loss raised more questions than any other. Ace reliever Bruce Sutter decided to cash in his free-agent status and put his split-fingered fastball on the open market. During the winter meetings, Sutter succumbed to an extravagant offer from the Atlanta Braves.

"The money's there," said Sutter. "I'd be a fool not to take it."

Sutter's loss caused concern. One of the top relief pitchers in the game, Sutter was coming off a 45-save season. It was Sutter who had struck out Gorman Thomas to clinch the World Series. Now the Cards would have to finish games without him.

Herzog still had one more major deal to make before the reporting date for spring training. On February 1, he landed out-fielder Jack Clark from San Francisco for pitcher Dave LaPoint, infielders Jose Gonzalez (who would later call himself Jose Uribe), and outfielder/first basemen David Green and Gary Rajsich.

Though Clark represented enormous talent, the trade contained negative elements. For one thing, the Cardinals were admitting they had failed to develop the talent they were seeking when they acquired Green. For another, the departure of LaPoint might weaken the club in an area that was already vulnerable—pitching.

A baseball man of conviction, Herzog viewed the trade differently. He thought it would help—a lot.

"I've been saying that we could finish anywhere from first to last," he said. "But now I'll tell you one thing—we won't finish last."

SPRING SCUTTLEBUTT

Loaded thus with questions, the Cardinals reported to their training base in St. Petersburg. Herzog contemplated a bullpen of Neil Allen, Jeff Lahti, Rick Horton, and Ken Dayley. Terry Pendleton, who

had hit .324 in 67 games, prepared for a season at third. Andy Van Slyke worked at first. Right-hander Bob Forsch, recovering from back surgery, gave some encouraging performances. Vince Coleman, a 23-year-old speedster who stole 101 bases at Louisville in 1984, appeared headed back to the minors.

The Cardinals remained a puzzle, and the standard spring training subterfuge reflected it. One rumor was that the Cards, rather than risk losing Ozzie Smith via free agency, would trade their superlative shortstop. It was an unsettling thought. With Smith catching everything in sight, the Cardinals might somehow find a way to contend. Without him, a successful season seemed unlikely.

The other spring scuttlebutt revolved around Herzog. If the team faltered from the gate, the speculation said, Herzog was gone. Such stories were not difficult to believe. Changes in the front office can often mean a change in managers.

The Cardinals had a lineup of questions and doubts, and the first pitch had not even been thrown.

2

FLYIN' HIGH

The Cardinals opened the 1985 season at Shea Stadium in New York. It was a big day for both teams, but bigger maybe for the Mets, who were unveiling Gary Carter, the catcher who they hoped would bring them from contention to the championship.

Carter was acquired in the off-season as part of a major deal—an old-fashioned blockbuster that took just about everyone by surprise. The Mets sent shortstop Hubie Brooks, catcher Mike Fitzgerald, centerfielder Herm Winningham, and pitcher Floyd Youmans to Montreal for Carter. He brought enthusiasm, power, and glamour. He would win games and sell tickets.

On Opening Day, the new Met centerpiece was in the starting lineup, batting cleanup, and Dwight Gooden, the 1984 Rookie of the Year, was on the mound.

Herzog made out the following starting lineup:

- Lonnie Smith, lf
- Tom Herr, 2b
- Terry Pendleton, 3b

- Jack Clark, 1b
- Darrell Porter, c
- Steve Braun, rf
- Andy Van Slyke, cf
- Ozzie Smith, ss
- Joaquin Andujar, p

The Cardinals had a centerpiece of their own. It was Jack Clark, who, in an 8-year stint with San Francisco, developed a reputation as one of the top hitters in baseball. He owned a .277 lifetime average, with 163 homers and 595 RBI.

A native of New Brighton, Pennsylvania, Clark entered the major leagues in 1975 and became a regular two years later. In 1978, he hit 25 homers and drove in 98 runs. In 1982, he hit 27 homers with 103 RBI.

Clark and San Francisco had formed an unhappy marriage, and it was no secret that the first baseman wanted out of Candlestick Park.

"I'm just not happy being here," he said. "I'm not going to ask for a trade . . . but it probably would be in the best interests of everybody if there was a change for me.

"Guys don't want to play for the Giants, and we don't go after free agents. I've had a hard time motivating myself this year because of what's been going on. I don't want to say bad things, but these are my feelings. I'm sorry if I hurt people's feelings, but I'd be lying to myself to hold them in.

"It's obvious I don't like playing at Candlestick and I feel betrayed, kind of, because it seems we're always rebuilding."

The 1984 season was Clark's last with the Giants. He was hitting .320 with 11 homers and 44 RBI when a cartilage tear in his right knee knocked him out on June 26. Thus, when he came to the Cardinals, he brought some uncertainty: would a change of scenery make him a happier and more effective ball player? Was his knee healthy? Would the vast expanse of Busch Stadium prove too much for his home-run stroke?

One factor was not disputed. If Clark was healthy and interested, he was a fine ball player. He would help. Maybe, as Herzog predicted, the Cardinals would not finish last.

When Jack Clark came to the Cards in 1985, he owned a lifetime .277 average with 163 homers and 595 RBI. It was just the beginning.

SEEKING A WIN

By the time Clark came to the plate for his new team on Opening Day, they trailed 2–0. After his first swing, the score was 2–1. He hit the ball well into the left-field bleachers.

All the same, the Cardinals lost. Joaquin Andujar did not have his best stuff and allowed five earned runs in five innings. Ken Dayley, Bill Campbell, and Andy Hassler pitched effectively in relief. Trailing 5–2, the Redbirds scored two in the seventh and one in the ninth to force the game to extra innings.

In the 10th, Carter gave the crowd of 46,781 the performance they had paid to see. He ripped Neil Allen's pitch over the left-field fence for a home run, giving the Mets a 6–5 victory. The season was under-

way, and the Cardinals were in last place.

After the traditional day off to allow for an Opening Day rainout, the Mets and the Cardinals collided again. The crowd fell to 18,864, although the competitive level remained high. John Tudor allowed one run and three hits in nine innings. Once again, the game entered extra innings, and once again, the Mets left Allen on the mound. Pendleton had driven in the only Cardinal run, and the Mets won it 2–1 in 11 innings. Sporting an 0–2 record, the Cardinals were at least undefeated in nine-inning games.

The next stop was Three Rivers Stadium in Pittsburgh. Having failed with Andujar and Tudor, St. Louis sent Kurt Kepshire against the Pirates. It was no contest. Pittsburgh scored four runs in the first inning

Clark takes a
shot in the leg
from Giant
pitcher Vida Blue.
He went on to
homer, single,
and drive in two
runs against his
former team as
the Cards beat
the Giants 9-4.

Clark may not be pleased that he was unable to pick off Ryne Sandberg, but he sure is pleased to be with the Redbirds.

"It's obvious I don't like playing at Candlestick," he said of his
former team, the San Francisco Giants.

Clark suffered knee damage in 1984, and St. Louis fans wondered if it would have an effect on his game. The answer was soon obvious.

In his first at-bat for the Cards, he drilled a home run into Shea Stadium's left-field bleachers. At left, he connects in Wrigley Field.

and eventually won 6–4. Willie McGee made his first start of the season, and drove home a run. In New York, the Mets beat Cincinnati 1–0. Four days into the season, the Cardinals were three games out of first place.

Pittsburgh proved inhospitable for the second straight day. The Pirates beat the Cardinals 4–3, with Tony Pena lifting a sacrifice fly in the eighth inning. Bill Campbell took the loss. In New York, the Mets beat Cincinnati again. Five days into the season, the Cardinals were four games out of first place. The bullpen had failed three out of four times. Where was Bruce Sutter? The Cards needed a win, and it was Andujar's turn to try for one.

DOMINICAN DYNAMITE

Before the seventh game of the 1982 World Series, a 29-year-old right-hander from the Dominican Republic spoke to St. Louis pitching coach Hub Kittle.

"He looked me in the eye and said, 'I am ready,' " said Kittle. "Before he walked out to the mound to start pitching, he said, 'This game is mine.' "

The pitcher was Joaquin Andujar, and the game indeed was his. Five days after being drilled below the right kneecap by a Ted Simmons line drive, Andujar beat the Milwaukee Brewers 6–3. In so doing, he showed his talent and determination. He also showed his temper.

In the seventh inning, Milwaukee's Jim Gantner bounced out to Andujar, then accused the pitcher of showing off. Before long, they were exchanging increasingly hostile words.

"I told him he was a hot dog," Gantner later said. "I said to him, 'You're a hot dog' and he said 'What?' I said to him again 'You're a hot dog' and that's when he turned and came after me. If I'd known he'd explode like that I would have called him that earlier."

"He called me a hot dog and something else," said Andujar. "I've got a hot temper and I'm not going to let anybody call me what he did."

Andujar came to the Cardinals on June 6, 1981, in a deal that sent Tony Scott to the Houston Astros. A native of San Pedro de Macoris, Dominican Republic, Andujar represented a curious blend of talent and temper. Maybe the Astros grew tired of waiting for him to develop. When they won the National League West in 1980, Andujar contributed only a 3–8 record with a 3.91 ERA.

With the Cardinals, he began to blossom immediately. After the trade, the 6', 180-pound right-hander went 6–1. In 1982, he enjoyed the best season of his career until that time, going 15–10 with a 2.47 ERA. Perhaps more than any other pitcher, he was responsible for the Cards' 1982 division title, going 5–0 in September.

Joaquin Andujar's temper is the driving force that makes him the outstanding pitcher he is.

A complicated individual, Andujar seems frustrated by a lack of recognition on one hand and a desire for privacy on the other. Baseball players with skills like his don't get both.

"One day, when I was sixteen years old and was starting out in professional baseball, my grandfather said to me, 'Grandson, don't you ever let anybody know who you are until the time comes. And then when the time comes, you will let them know.' "

Andujar has indeed let them know. They certainly know that he's awfully tough to hit. In 1984, he was the only 20-game winner in the National League.

In 1985, Andujar would find controversy again. He would refuse to attend the All-Star Game in Minneapolis, quarreling with National League manager Dick Williams. With a 15–3 record, Andujar believed he automatically deserved a start in the game. Williams had intended to name a

A native of San Pedro de Marcoris, Dominican Republic, Andujar lives by a piece of advice given him by his grandfather: "Don't let anybody know who you are until the time comes. When the time comes, you will let them know."

starter after watching a duel between the Padres' right-hander LaMarr Hoyt and Andujar.

Controversy aside, Andujar is still one of baseball's toughest competitors on the mound. And on April 14, when the Cardinals needed a victory, Joaquin Andujar gave them one. He scattered seven hits over seven innings, allowing one run. In addition, he collected two hits and drove home two runs.

Jack Clark hit his second home run of the season, and Terry Pendleton and Willie McGee had two hits apiece. McGee earned the game-winning RBI as the Cards scored twice in the first inning, eventually beating the Pirates 10–4. They were tied with Philadelphia for last place, but at last they had their first victory. They were also going home.

THE THIEF

One bright spot was beginning to shine for the Cards in April—rookie Vince Coleman. When he joined the team on April 18, the team was 2–5. And then things began to happen.

When a team wins a pennant, people invariably ask about the "turning point." For the 1984 Detroit Tigers, it occurred in spring training, when they acquired reliever Willie Hernandez in a trade. In 1979, the Pittsburgh Pirates began their rush when they traded for third baseman Bill Madlock. The 1982 Cardinals built their surge around excellent September pitching.

For the 1985 Redbirds, little debate can take place on the "turning point." It came the day that Vince Coleman played his first game.

Coleman was born on September 22, 1961, in Jacksonville, Florida. A 6', 170-pound switch-hitting outfielder, he was the 10th pick in the regular phase of the June 1982 free-agent draft. He rose quickly

When Dick Williams didn't make Andujar the automatic starter in the All-Star game, the pitcher refused to attend.

Vince Coleman's arrival in St. Louis triggered a change in the Cardinals' luck.

through the farm system, leaving astounding feats behind him.

In his first pro season, he stole seven bases in one game for Johnson City of the Appalachian League. One year later, he stole 145 bases, a pro baseball record, despite missing 31 games with an injury. Graduating to the American Association in 1984, Coleman continued to develop, setting a league record of 101 steals and making the All-Star team.

"HE KNOWS HOW TO RUN"

That Coleman meshed with the Cardinals' reliance on speed would be a gross understatement. When he joined the club, the Cardinals had lost five of their first seven games. They introduced him on April 18, leading off and playing center. He went 1 for 3 and stole his first two bases as the Cardinals dropped a 7–1 decision to the

Montreal Expos. Almost immediately thereafter, the ball club began to improve.

Coleman needed to make some slight adjustments. He was, on occasion, getting picked off at first base. It didn't take him long to learn, though. And he impressed another great St. Louis base stealer—Lou Brock.

"He knows how to run and when to run," said Brock. "Sometimes you forget his in-

experience. Probably the only thing he has left to learn is where to run. Around the base paths there is a fast track and a slow track."

What struck Brock the most was the size

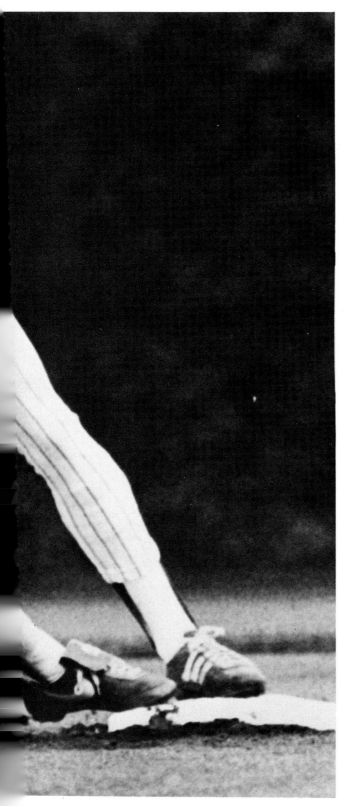

of Coleman's lead.

"You've got your own comfort zone that exists a certain length from the base in which you can do pretty much what you want," said Brock.

The master thief also described a neutral zone that the pitcher and runner share.

"Then there's the pitcher's zone," Brock said. "Vince is in the pitcher's zone all the time."

As Herzog began to enjoy the show, news of Coleman's talent spread almost as quickly as he covered ground. In Atlanta, the grounds crew poured so much water

Lou Brock, the master base thief of all time, says of Coleman's ability to steal: "He knows how to run and when to run. You forget his inexperience." Sometimes speed can get you in trouble, though. Below, Coleman gets caught in a rundown.

**News of Coleman's talent spread quickly: one team watered down the area around
first base so much that the
rookie asked, "Why don't you
put a bridge over that thing?"**

**Coleman tries to slam on the
brakes, but Cub Jody Davis
gets him for the out.**

around first base that Coleman asked, "Why don't you put a bridge over that thing."

The story was reminiscent of a 1962 meeting between the Los Angeles Dodgers and the San Francisco Giants. Dodger Maury Wills stole 104 bases, leading the Giants to hose down the base path around first.

"Hey, Alvin," the Dodgers needled Giant manager Alvin Dark. "What time does the tide come in?"

Coleman did more than simply steal bases. In an April series against the Mets, he beat out a routine ground ball to second base. His speed unnerved opponents. Soon, the scouts became believers.

"They have so much speed," said one scout of the new Cardinals. "They not only beat you, they intimidate you."

In Coleman's second game in the majors, he went 4 for 5 with a double and triple as the Cards beat Pittsburgh 5–4. He went 2 for 3 with three stolen bases in a 6–0 whitewash of Pittsburgh on April 21. Three days later, he was 1 for 4 and stole his sixth base to help the Cards reach the .500 mark in a 5–1 victory over the Mets.

It had taken the Cardinals almost three weeks into the season to achieve mediocrity. Having finally reached the .500 level, they then lost four in a row. They would still have good days and bad. With Coleman around, though, they would never be the same club.

THE WIZARD OF OZ

Since the middle of the 19th century, when baseball began to flourish, thousands of men have played shortstop.

They came in great variety. Some were tall, like 6'2" Marty Marion. Others were smaller, though perhaps not so small as 5'6" Phil Rizzuto. Some were rugged, like the great Honus Wagner, scooping up earth with the ball. Some could hit, like the great Ernie Banks, with his 512 career home runs. Many, many more were con-

When baseball history recalls the most awesome shortstops, Ozzie Smith will certainly be at the top of the list.

signed to the minors by the phrase, "Good field, no hit."

What all of these men had in common, however, was a battle against the excruciating demands of the position. A shortstop should be quick enough to cover ground both to his left and right. He must be alert on the hopper past the pitcher, and be able to sprint into the outfield for a pop up.

The fine shortstop has a strong arm, so that when he backhands a ball in short left field, he can deliver the ball to first in time to catch the batter. He must have courage to tag base runners, and the agility to avoid their slides on the double play.

Shortstop tends to attract the very best athletes. The talented Little Leaguer will either pitch or play short. So will the skilled high school player. Even in profes-

No, it's not a new way to field the ball. Ozzie is doing backflips over his new five- **year contract that made him the highest paid shortstop in major-league history.**

sional ball, the position remains crucial. A ball club cannot win without strength up the middle, and many a pitcher has been grateful for the defensive effort registered by a shortstop.

Considering the number of people who have played the position and the talent the position attracts, it would be a mark of deepest respect to anoint someone the greatest fielding shortstop in history.

And yet, on February 10, 1982, the St. Louis Cardinals acquired a man about whom this very claim can be made. His name is Ozzie Smith, he hailed from Mobile, Alabama, and he played shortstop so well that eventually they took his name and formed a tribute of it. They called him the "Wizard of Oz."

Osborne Earl Smith was born on December 26, 1954. He played college ball at California State Poly, and spent a year in the minors at Walla Walla. As a member of

the San Diego Padre organization, Smith didn't have to wait long for his shot at the big leagues: the Padres made him their regular shortstop in 1978.

In four years with San Diego, he never hit higher than .258, but his reputation as a fielder grew. He could, it seemed, do everything. His trademarks were acrobatic leaps and bounces that enabled him to get to difficult balls, then throw quickly. One of his favorite maneuvers was to bounce up immediately after leaping for a ball, thus being in position to make his play. Smith made his first All-Star team in 1981, but had long before caught the attention of Whitey Herzog.

The Cardinals had soured on Garry Templeton, who had once been considered an untouchable as far as trades were concerned. Rumors flew and persisted. Finally, on February 10, 1982, the trade came. Templeton went to San Diego,

Smith's value isn't only appreciated by the Cards: as a starter in both the 1984 and 1985 All-Star games, the shortstop played the entire nine innings of both, despite the presence of great power hitters on the teams.

"I always work hard at what I do," says the Wizard, "and try to give the people who come to the ballpark their money's worth."

where he later helped the Padres win a National League pennant.

Smith came to St. Louis, where he immediately helped the Cardinals win a World Series. He won ovations on a regular basis, led NL shortstops in fielding percentage, won his third straight Gold Glove, and led the league in assists for the fourth straight year.

He also adapted quickly to the artificial surface at Busch Stadium, notching his best average in four years and posting the highest doubles total of his career until then. He hit .556 in the 1982 playoffs against Atlanta, then set a seven-game World Series record for putouts by a shortstop with 22.

A measure of Smith's value, both real and perceived, comes from the people who know best—the managers. In both 1984 and '85, Smith played the entire All-Star game. Despite the presence of great power hitters, Smith nevertheless was the one who was deemed by the managers as being necessary for victory.

As the 1985 training camp proceeded, however, you had to wonder about Smith's future. He was eligible to become a free agent at the end of the year, and that created a dilemma for the Cardinals. They either had to sign him, or risk losing him when his old contract expired.

The Cardinals were sure of one thing: they definitely did not want to lose Ozzie Smith the same way they lost Bruce Sutter. Two such massive losses in successive years would have crippled the franchise. Yes, they would either sign him, or trade him. Smith recognized the possibility.

During the spring, he was asked about the possibility of a trade: "It's part of the game." He did not want it to happen, though.

As insurance against such a loss, the team acquired two other shortstops: veteran Ivan DeJesus and minor-league fielding whiz Jose Oquendo.

"I think that they are telling me one thing, and that's that I may not be here that much longer," Smith said after the acquisition of DeJesus.

Both Smith and Herzog wished the situation to be resolved one way or the other, and quickly. "For morale purposes, it's not a good situation," Herzog said.

One week after the season began, the Cardinals signed Smith. They had tied him up for another five years.

The announcement was made at a news conference that included August A. Busch, Jr., the venerable brewery owner and head of the club.

"This is a great day for me today," Busch said in his rare appearance. "It's my pleasure to announce that Ozzie Smith will be wearing a Cardinal uniform for the next five years."

The lucrative contract caused a puzzling wave of resentment in a press that never blinked when other stars received huge amounts. How people failed to recognize Smith's value to his team was a mystery.

"I never set out to be the highest-paid player," Smith said. "I always work hard at what I do, and try to give people who come to the ballpark their money's worth."

A SHINING ALL-STAR

Over the first few weeks of the season, one thing about the Cardinals became apparent: second baseman Tom Herr was playing a healthy style of ball for someone who had undergone three knee operations. He collected four hits in the opening series against New York and never slowed down after that.

Thomas Mitchell Herr was born in Lancaster, Pennsylvania, on April 4, 1956. He

For someone who has undergone three knee operations, Tommy Herr is sure playing healthy baseball.

signed with the St. Louis organization as a free agent on August 2, 1974. He worked his way up the Cardinal farm system, playing at Johnson City, St. Petersburg, Arkansas, and Springfield before making his major-league debut in 1979.

Herr came to the majors to stay in 1980, batting .248 in 76 games. As he matured and became the regular second baseman, his talents proved diverse. For one thing, he was a switch-hitter. He led National League second basemen in assists, double plays, and fielding percentage in 1981. He showed a knack for stealing a base, and was third on the club in RBI.

In 1982, Herr delivered a fine season despite the onset of injury problems. He hit .266 and was second on the club in runs and stolen bases. He hit only .160 in the World Series, but drove in five runs. He set a Series record in Game 4 when two runners scored on his long sacrifice fly.

"It's not like this is something new," said Herzog of his second baseman's emergence as a star in 1985.

Ryne Sandberg beats Herr to the bag on a steal, but Herr stole the starting All-Star role from Sandberg.

Herr played the World Series with injury problems, and in November 1982, underwent arthroscopic surgery on his right knee to repair damaged cartilage. He then hurt his left knee while working on an exercise machine in spring training, requiring more arthroscopic surgery.

After going on medical rehabilitation at Arkansas, Herr returned to the Cardinals and hit .323. By August, however, his left knee needed more work and the ensuing surgery knocked him out for the entire 1983 season.

If 1984 was a test, then Herr passed easily. He led the league in double plays, proving he could still pivot despite the knee problems. He finished second to Ryne Sandberg in fielding percentage and had 42 multiple-hit games.

He was back.

In 1981, Herr led National League second basemen in assists, double plays, and fielding percentage.

Herr has kept the Redbirds flying high in '85.

As the Cardinals struggled early in '85, Herr's bat found the ball. He went 3 for 3 against Pittsburgh on April 13 . . . drove in three runs against the Pirates on April 19 . . . went 3 for 5 with a stolen base and an RBI against Montreal on April 26 . . . went 3 for 5 with a triple against Los Angeles on April 30. . . .

After 40 games, Herr led the league with a .385 average. He and Jack Clark were both driving in runs. Herr credited experience and the presence of Clark. Herzog credited Herr.

"It's not like this is something new," said the manager, pointing out that Herr had entered the season with a respectable .276 average. With all due apologies to the skipper, it was new. Doing it over 40 games would not be enough, though. No one would mind if Herr wound up at .300 for the season.

April had indeed been a shaky month. But things were beginning to gel, and for the Redbirds, the race had just begun.

3

MANAGING A MIRACLE

Some baseball people caution against placing too much value on April and September performances. The theory is simple. In April, statistics are muddled by a variety of factors. Rookie enthusiasm inflates performance for a while. Rain and off-days detract from continuity. Veterans are still feeling their way. In September, except for the contenders and the spoilers, the games represent a chance for young players to show what they can do. The veterans are tired. Most teams are making plans for next year.

In a sense, then, the baseball season doesn't begin until May. By then, the rookies are learning about the big leagues, the veterans are working into shape, the weather is clearing up, and the ball clubs settle into the timelessness of the season.

This time can bring a pleasant limbo. A team can move along, playing neither poorly nor well, without affecting its pennant chances very much. A pretender can continue to pretend, the contender can search for its chemistry.

The only formula is to stay close. A

manager knows that the season is long, and he wants above all for his team to be there when the pennant races begin shaping up many weeks ahead. He learns about his pitching, finds out about his bench. Some of the best managing is done here.

SURVIVING STORMS

Whitey Herzog knows all about the length of the season. He has been around baseball a long time. Herzog broke into the majors in 1956 with the Washington Senators. He was living in a trailer at the time.

"We have a good-sized bedroom, a kitchen, shower, washer, stove, and all the modern conveniences," he said then.

A left-handed bat and arm, Herzog was a product of the New York Yankee farm system. He hit .245 in his rookie season, bounced around the majors until 1963, serving with Kansas City, Baltimore, and Detroit. In Baltimore, he played under Paul Richards, who was creating an organization built on pitching and defense.

Herzog stole only 13 bases in his career,

(Above) **Whitey's penchant for trading and reorganizing may not have been popular at one point, but he and his jackrabbits have Cardinal fans thinking differently now.**

a minute total for someone who would later manage Vince Coleman.

He loved to play, though. In 1960, Kansas City manager Bob Elliott watched Herzog grimace while pursuing a fly ball.

"That leg is paining him," said Elliott, referring to an old injury of Herzog's. "But he never would tell me if I didn't ask him."

Herzog had more to offer than desire, though. He had an instinct for the game. When his playing days were through, he quickly found a job. He did some scouting for Kansas City and in 1966 joined the New York Mets in the front office. The Mets won the World Series in 1969. It may have been more than coincidence.

When Texas owner Bob Short hired Herzog to manage the Rangers in 1972, he said, "He developed one of the most formidable minor-league systems in baseball."

Herzog never finished the season in Texas, being relieved of command on September 9. He eventually wound up in Kansas City, where he won divisional titles for three years straight, starting in 1976. Herzog was fired after the 1979 season, but he knew better than to worry. As he once had said, "I'll never be out of work, that's for sure. Someone will always hire me. I believe that."

In 1980, the Cardinals became the lucky recipient of Herzog's baseball knowledge. Over the 73 games he managed that year, the Redbirds went 38–35. He moved up to general manager in August, and later hired himself back as manager. "Every manager I was thinking about, I couldn't get," he said.

The new general manager made every player except shortstop Garry Templeton available for a trade; then, with characteristic frankness, he named his priority.

"We need three kinds of pitchers," he said. "Right-handers, left-handers, and relievers."

So saying, Herzog entered the wild winter of 1980–81. It was time, as Leo Durocher had once said, to back up the truck.

Whitey's arsenal of coaches: (opposite page, right) **Mike Roarke,** (clockwise, starting above left) **Nick Levya, Red Schoendienst, Dave Ricketts,** and **Hal Lanier.**

Herzog's attack on the base paths has been led by Vince Coleman, who paves the way for the rest of the jackrabbits. Said one scout, "They have so much speed, they not only beat you, they intimidate you."

Herzog began to trade, and he energetically rebutted any criticism they generated.

"People didn't understand that a lot of things had to be done," he said. "Guys here didn't like each other. There were four different cliques in the clubhouse."

By the time Herzog was finished trading, the organization contained fewer cliques and more potential. Winning baseball returned to St. Louis, and UPI gave Herzog the credit, naming him baseball's Executive of the Year both in 1981 and '82.

IN THE RUNNING

The Cardinals entered May of 1985 with an 8–11 record, and the team floundered for a while. It won a couple, then lost a couple. A few things happened. First, they survived their first trip to the West Coast, emerging with a 4–3 record. They won a game when Dodger first baseman Greg Brock made two errors in the 10th inning. Second, on May 17, they traded Lonnie Smith to Kansas City. Then, on Sunday, May 19, they lost to Houston 7–3 to fall three games under .500 and 7½ games from the lead.

When May ended, the Cardinals stood at 24–21, four games behind the division-leading Mets. They had won eight of their last 10 games, and they had done their job. They had stayed close.

In watching the standings, you couldn't help but notice. The primitive beginnings of a pennant race were forming and the St. Louis Cardinals were very much in the running.

4
OFF TO THE RACES

The Cards had improved dramatically since April, but there was still a big question mark: would the pitching hold up?

For instance, John Tudor, the left-hander obtained by the Cardinals for slugger George Hendrick, was lurching along with a 1–7 record. Then came a call from a friend, and a subsequent change in fortune.

Tudor, who had not won since May 3, took the mound on June 3 and pitched the Cardinals to a 9–5 victory over the Houston Astros. He then credited a friend who had telephoned him after detecting a flaw on television.

"A friend called and something good came out of it," said Tudor. "In my delivery I have a pause where I've kept my leg up. Everything comes together then. It allows my arms to catch up with my legs. That's where my problem was. I'd lost that in what I call my gathering point.

"It seems like a silly thing, but it's an important part of my delivery. I worked on it and felt fine tonight."

The Cardinals were moving. In that victory over the Astros, Jack Clark hit his 11th homer. Vince Coleman stole two more bases for a total of 36. Herr drove in two runs, and Andy Van Slyke went 3 for 3. The Mets lost in Los Angeles, so the Redbirds pulled within five games of first place.

More important, Tudor's victory triggered a string over which St. Louis won 15 of 19 games, with Tudor collecting five of those victories. Furthermore, the streak included three triumphs in a four-game series against the Mets in New York.

On June 9, Terry Pendleton hit an inside-the-park grand slam and Joaquin Andujar notched his 11th victory to give the Cards an 8–2 victory and a split of their doubleheader.

Suddenly, it was time for the Cards to surge: Danny Cox pitched a four-hitter and drove in two runs on June 10 . . . Tudor upped his record to 4–7 on Friday the 13th . . . Andujar struggled to his 12th victory, as the Cards outlasted Chicago 11–10 . . . St. Louis slipped into third place as the Mets faltered in a series against Montreal.

On June 18, Tudor made it 5–7 with a 6–

John Tudor had posted a meager 1–7 record when a friend pointed out a flaw in his delivery.

Third baseman Terry Pendleton thrilled Cardinal fans with his inside-the-park grand slam on June 9 against the Mets.

2 victory over Philadelphia, pulling the Cardinals within a half-game of first place. Two days later, Willie McGee collected his seventh game-winning RBI in a 5–0 victory over Philadelphia. On June 23, before a crowd of 45,881, Tudor notched his fifth straight victory, blanking the Cubs 7–0. He hurled a two-hitter and had two hits with the game-winning RBI.

"I like to chip in with a base hit now and then," he said. "I've had a three-hit game before. I just swing at it. I can hit it."

For the Cubs, it was the 12th straight loss. They found little comfort from Whitey Herzog.

"I don't have any sympathy for them because I can't," he said. "I feel for them. I've been down that road before. I know what it's like."

The Cardinals had traveled a different road for the last 19 games. Now they would cool off. But they would never be far from the lead. They had the look of a contender.

DANNY COX

John Tudor wasn't the only pitcher who heated up in June; Danny Cox was starting to look pretty good. A native of Northhampton, England, Cox needed only 15 weeks to pass through every classification in the Cardinals' farm chain and make it to the majors.

He blossomed in time to help the Cardinals make a run for the pennant. While Joaquin Andujar and John Tudor were pitching the club into contention, Cox was right there with them. There were times, in fact, when he was the most impressive of the three.

Cox was signed as the 12th selection in the regular phase of the June 1981 free-agent draft. He went 9–4 for Johnson City in 1981, making the Appalachian League All-Star team. While the Cardinals were winning the '82 World Series, he went 5–3 for Springfield, earning a berth on the Midwest League All-Star squad.

By the time Pendleton comes down, Cub Gary Woods will be safe. Pendleton was leaping for Andy Van Slyke's throw from right field.

Danny Cox whipped
through the entire
Cardinal farm system
in only 15 weeks.

Cox flirted with a perfect game in May
when he pitched 7$\frac{2}{3}$ perfect innings
against the Reds. The right-hander
finished with a two-hit, 5-0 victory.

Kurt Kepshire has
been the solid fourth
starter in the Redbirds'
rotation.

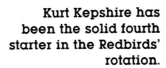

Kepshire cocks his arm and prepares to fire against the Cubs on a rainy day in Chicago.

All-Star terms are nice, progress is better. Progress accelerated in 1983.

Cox started at St. Petersburg with a 2–2 record in five games, went to Arkansas, where he was 8–3 in 11 starts and made the Texas League All-Star team. He then landed in Louisville before being summoned to the Cardinals.

A 6'4", 230-pound right-hander with a penchant for throwing strikes, Cox started the 1984 season with St. Louis, was returned to Louisville, and rejoined the majors for good, going 6–3 in 13 starts the rest of the way.

On May 31, Cox flirted with the most spectacular of pitching feats, going 7⅔ perfect innings against the Cincinnati Reds. He finished with a two-hit, 5–0 victory that jumped his record to 6–1. Before a crowd of 32,397 on June 20, he fired another 5–0 victory, this time beating Philadelphia to up his mark to 9–2.

On the final day of June, Cox pitched nine innings, allowing one unearned run to help the Cardinals score a 2–1, 11-inning triumph over the Mets. Jack Clark hit his 15th home run, and Vince Coleman drove in the winning run and stole his 52nd base. A crowd of 47,425 watched as the race got hotter.

5
MIDSEASON MAGIC

The Dodgers were in town, and what could be more American than baseball in St. Louis on the Fourth of July? The city on the banks of the Mississippi is a historic one, representing the commerce up and down the river as well as the gateway to the West.

It has seen its share of baseball, too. A charter member of the National League, the Cardinals have operated continuously in the NL since 1892. They were known in 1892 as the Browns, then became the Perfectos. In 1899, the Perfectos became the Cardinals.

The franchise has won 13 pennants and nine World Series. Some of the greatest players, managers, and executives in the history of the game have toiled for the organization: Grover Cleveland Alexander, Jake Beckley, Jim Bottomley, Roger Bresnahan, Lou Brock, Mordecai "Three Fingers" Brown, Jesse Burkett, Roger Connor, Dizzy Dean, Frankie Frisch, Pud Galvin, Bob Gibson, Burleigh Grimes, Chick Hafey, Jesse Haines, Rogers Hornsby, Miller Huggins, Rabbitt Maranville, John Mc-

Graw, Bill McKechnie, Ducky Medwick, Johnny Mize, Stan Musial, Kid Nichols, Branch Rickey, Enos Slaughter, Dazzy Vance, Hoyt Wilhelm, and Cy Young are all Hall of Famers who labored for the Cardinals.

The Cardinals have been involved in some of the most exciting moments in World Series history:

- In 1926, the aging Grover Alexander won the second and sixth games against the New York Yankees, then was summoned from the bullpen in Game 7. He struck out Tony Lazzeri with the bases loaded, and the Cardinals won the game and the Series.
- In 1934, the "Gas House Gang" won the NL pennant on the last day of the season, then defeated the Detroit Tigers in seven games. Ducky Medwick was ejected from the famous seventh game when he collided with Detroit third baseman Marvin Owen, prompting angry Tiger fans to toss garbage at him. Medwick was ejected to halt the

disturbance and allow the Cardinals to complete their 11–0 victory.

- The only all–St. Louis Series came in 1944, when the Cardinals defeated the Browns, 4 games to 2. It was the only pennant ever won by the Browns, who moved and became the Baltimore Orioles in 1954.
- Two years later, Enos Slaughter made his famous dash from first base to home with the winning run. With the score tied 3–3 in the eighth inning of the deciding game, Slaughter was on first. He scored on Harry Walker's single to left center, surprising Boston relay man Johnny Pesky, who hesitated before throwing home.
- In 1964, Bob Gibson won two games, Ken Boyer hit a grand slam to win Game 4, and Tim McCarver broke up Game 5 with a home run. The Cardinals beat the Yankees, 4 games to 3.
- Gibson and Lou Brock controlled the 1967 World Series, as the Cardinals ended Boston's Impossible Dream, 4 games to 3. Gibson pitched three complete game victories. Brock hit .414 and set a Series record by stealing seven bases. A familiar World Series performer, Roger Maris, hit .385 for the Cards.
- In 1982, for the seventh time in their history, the Cardinals prevailed in a seven-game series. Darrell Porter won the series MVP Award, but Joaquin Andujar and George Hendrick are deserving also.

On July 4, 1985, the Cardinals celebrated the traditional halfway mark of the season sitting in first place. They also beat the Dodgers 3–2. Joaquin Andujar raised his record to a major-league-leading 14-3, but it was Vince Coleman who provided the excitement with a strong defensive play. In the ninth inning, the Dodgers' Terry Whitfield lined a fastball off the left-field wall and began what he thought was an easy cruise toward a sure double. Coleman barehanded the ball off the wall, threw to

second baseman Tom Herr, and Whitfield was tagged out.

"I feel real excited about it," said Coleman. "I felt like I do when I steal a base. It was electrifying. Ozzie always says one play comes along and you often win or lose because of that one play. That play stuck out in this game. I will tingle with excitement all night because of this."

Los Angeles manager Tommy Lasorda thought Whitfield was safe, though he gave the Cardinals credit for their succession of defensive plays.

"It was a great game to win but a tough one to lose," said Lasorda. "It was a heckuva game. It was great for the spectators."

The Cardinals made defense their theme

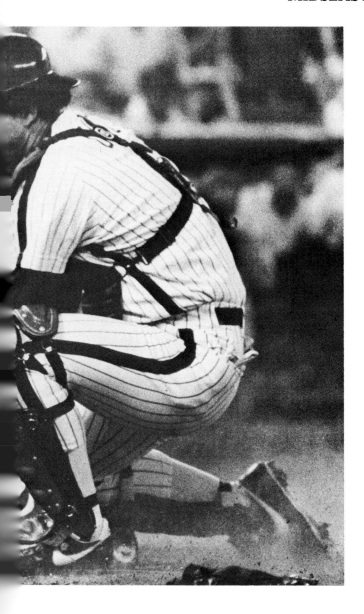

The scene was 1982 when catcher Darrell Porter took the World Series MVP honor as the Cards beat the Brewers in seven games. But 1985 has been a tough season for the veteran catcher, who spent a good deal of time on the disabled list. Fortunately, he was healthy for that last push in September.

throughout the game. In the sixth inning, the Dodgers had three walks, an error, and a hit, but did not score. In the big play, St. Louis catcher Tom Nieto, who had two hits to drive in two runs, including the game-winner, cut down Ken Landreaux attempting to steal second.

"That was the play of the game," said Andujar. "They could have, and should have, scored three or four runs that inning. Tommy made a great throw."

In the seventh inning, Andujar loaded the bases with one out. He struck out Landreaux, but Pedro Guerrero hit a rising shot toward left field. Third baseman Terry Pendleton made a leaping stab and caught the ball, saving two runs.

"It was a tough play," said Pendleton. "You try to follow the crack of the ball but the crowd noise was such you couldn't hear well. I just timed the jump and got it. The key was the timing. I went up as high as I could."

The contribution by Nieto was particularly gratifying, since regular catcher Darrell Porter was on the disabled list for the second time in the season. Nieto was doing a superb job as a reserve. On July 7, he drove in two more runs, including another game-winner, to give the Cardinals a 7–1 victory over the Dodgers.

The contribution was overlooked a bit because Tudor continued his remarkable pitching, raising his record to 9–7. Never-

Terry Pendleton's theory on fielding: "You try to follow the crack of the ball. I just time the ball and get it. The key is timing."

theless, Nieto had been producing. It was his fifth game-winning hit of the season. A week earlier, he had driven home the decider against the Mets.

At the halfway point, the Cardinals led the division by 1½ games over second-place Montreal. They had come a long way since Gary Carter's Opening-Day homer. However, the crucial weeks of summer loomed. Much work remained for Whitey Herzog and his rapid Redbirds.

BULLPEN BY COMMITTEE

As the Cards flew toward the All-Star break, the pressure on the bullpen increased. Relievers are permitted few, if any, deviations from effectiveness. On one hand, they must walk nobody. On the

Catcher Tom Nieto was superb as he filled in for regular catcher Darrell Porter.

other, they certainly must not allow home runs. It is their task to work within this peculiar dilemma every day. Often they have to do it with the bases loaded.

For the most part, the relief pitcher is even denied the luxury of creating his own mess. His assignment is to clean up someone else's mess. One minute, the bullpen specialist is relaxing in the sun. The next minute, he is warming up as disaster gathers in wait for him on the field. He walks in to face a Gary Carter or a Pedro Guerrero—it always seems to be one or the other.

Cardinal pitchers were accustomed to the pressure, however. They had felt it over the winter, from the first moment Bruce Sutter departed for Atlanta. With his farewell, their role became clear: they were the key to the season. If they pitched well, the Cardinals might contend. If not, they wouldn't.

Herzog never really expected to develop a super reliever. Instead, he hoped to fashion a flexible, deep bullpen that could give him 30 saves. In a "Bullpen by Committee," the Cardinals might overcome the loss of Sutter.

The bullpen, if all proceeded well, would consist of right-handers Neil Allen and Jeff Lahti, and left-handers Ricky Horton and Ken Dayley. Bill Campbell, not on the winter roster but destined to make the club, would also contribute.

Allen shouldered the most pressure. Having been the unfortunate player obtained from New York in exchange for Keith Hernandez, Allen was a highly visible Cardinal. Projecting their hope that perhaps he could justify the deal, people imagined Allen as the man to fill Sutter's absence.

It was a difficult position and Allen never really made it. Before long, the rest of the bullpen was ahead of him. He was finally traded to the Yankees during the All-Star break.

The rest of the bullpen fared better. By late August, the Cardinals would be tied for third in the league in saves.

Dayley, born on February 25, 1959, in

Ken Dayley was the Atlanta Braves' first pick in the 1980 draft, but he didn't blossom until he was acquired by the Cardinals.

Rick Horton, ranked among the Cards' most effective starters in 1984, became a situation reliever in 1985, used either to retire a lefty batter or to set up the short relief man.

Jeff Lahti, formerly Sutter's set-up man, began to save games for himself.

Bill Campbell, a 12-year veteran, led the league in saves in 1977.

Jerome, Idaho, never became what the Atlanta Braves hoped when they made him their number 1 pick in the June 1980 draft. He helped the Cardinals in a three-game weekend series against the Mets in June. On that Friday night, he nailed down John Tudor's seventh win for his sixth save. On Sunday, he was the winning pitcher in a 2–1 triumph to up his record to 2–0.

Horton, from Poughkeepsie, New York, ranked among the Cardinals' most effective starters in 1984, despite switching off between starting and relief. As a reliever, he was 1–0, as a starter 8–4. On the 1985 staff, however, Horton became a situation reliever, used either to retire a left-handed batter or to set up the short-relief man.

The biggest name in the bullpen was a man who had labored well for the Cardinals without much credit. Jeff Lahti came to the Cardinals on April 1, 1982, as part of a deal that sent Bob Shirley to Cincinnati. A 6' right-hander from Oregon City, Oregon, Lahti relies on a double-play ball

or a strikeout to escape a jam. Formerly used as a set-up man for Sutter, Lahti responded to the challenge of closing games himself.

With the Cardinals approaching the All-Star break, Lahti registered back-to-back saves against the San Diego Padres. On Saturday, he closed out Danny Cox's 11th victory with 1⅓ perfect innings for his eighth save. On Sunday, he nailed down Kurt Kepshire's seventh triumph by getting one out.

Bill Campbell entered the season with 119 lifetime saves. A veteran of 12 major-league seasons, the right-hander was no longer the pitcher he had been in 1977 when he led the league with 31 saves. Nevertheless, he came in a trade with the Phillies, pitched well early, and continued to provide steady pitching. Not used in save situations, Campbell instead helped set up the rest of the bullpen to close the game.

The bullpen received help from still

Bob Forsch came back from surgery in 1984 to provide solid relief in 1985.

another individual, Bob Forsch. He had been a starter—and a good one—for most of his career. He had experienced back pain, and finally surgery, in 1984. His career had been in doubt. Yet here he was, getting an occasional outing, making a big start.

Robert Herbert Forsch, born on January 13, 1950, came to the big leagues in 1974, when he went 7–4. For years, he was one of the Cardinals' most dependable starters, notching at least 10 victories eight times in nine seasons.

On April 16, 1978, he started his season by firing a no-hitter in beating Philadelphia 5–0. It was the first National League no-hitter in St. Louis since July 17, 1924, when Jesse Haines throttled the Boston Braves. (Casey Stengel made the last out in that game.)

Forsch said he heard radio broadcasters discussing the developing no-hitter when he entered the Cardinal clubhouse between innings to stay warm from the chilly, 43-degree weather.

"They were saying a no-hitter hadn't been thrown here since 1924," he said. "And the guys on the bench stopped talking about it in the eighth inning. But I didn't mind talking about it. A pitcher knows what's going on out on the field.

"Heck, I was born Friday the 13th. I can't be too superstitious."

With key contributions from a man who had been born on Friday the 13th, the Cardinals were enjoying good fortune in 1985. Forsch pitched a complete game victory on April 15. He made it 2–0 six days later, pitching six shutout innings to beat Pittsburgh. He pitched one key relief inning against Houston on May 17 in a game the Cardinals rallied to win 8–6. He established himself as a weapon ready when needed.

WANDERING WEST

The Cardinals arrived at the All-Star break with a 2½-game lead and tantalizing prospects. Immediately after the break, they would proceed to the West Coast. If they did well there, if they came back with the lead, then perhaps they were serious contenders. With half a season to go, anything could happen.

6

"THE BEST IN OUR LEAGUE"

Blame the Pacific Time Zone. Blame the beaches. Or the weather, the palm trees, the guacamole salad, or perhaps even the ball clubs out there. No one knows exactly why, but a trip to the West Coast usually provides a test for Eastern and Midwest teams.

Now the Cardinals were facing their most challenging safari of the year. Four games in Los Angeles. Three in San Francisco. Four in San Diego. Then three in Chicago. On this trip, they would learn a little about themselves. Maybe too much.

The trip started poorly. Joaquin Andujar, Danny Cox, and John Tudor all started games in Dodger Stadium and none could win. The Cards were 0–3 on a trip that was supposed to measure their strength as a contender. Then they assembled an effort that demonstrated many of their gifts.

Kurt Kepshire showed his value as a fourth starter by pitching seven strong innings. Vince Coleman stole a base. Steve Braun hit a pinch-hit home run. Whitey Herzog used his "Bullpen by Committee," and it produced a win and a save. The

Cardinals beat the Dodgers 4–2 in 10 innings. It was an important win, but Herzog nevertheless worried about the Cardinal attack.

"Their [Dodger] pitching was absolutely super. They shut us down completely," Herzog said. "If you take away the two runs we scored in the 10th inning [on Braun's homer], we only scored five runs in four games."

Herzog used Ken Dayley, rookie Joe Boever, Jeff Lahti, Ricky Horton, and Bob Forsch to generate the victory.

In San Francisco, things went much better, thanks to the continued efforts of Steve Braun. He singled home the tie-breaking run in the eighth, giving Joaquin Andujar a 4–3 victory over the Giants. Braun was hitting for Andujar, and swung at a 3–0 pitch.

"I expect the green light on 3–0," said Braun. "One key for me was that I laid off two pitches that were down. If I had been too aggressive, I probably just would have bounced out to second base. I had a good feeling before I went up yesterday and

67

after I hit that homer it increased my confidence level."

Herzog still wondered about the Cardinals' relative lack of offense.

"I just wish we would start scoring a little earlier in the game so we would not have to keep winning this way," said Herzog.

But winning this way would lead to other ways.

The next day belonged to Darrell Porter. After suffering from an injury and a lack of production in the first half of the season, he was back in the lineup and delivering. He collected two hits and two RBI, hit a home run, and notched the game-winning RBI in the Cardinal 6–3 victory over the Giants. Danny Cox went the distance to raise his record to 12–5. Willie McGee collected three hits, Andy Van Slyke stole a base. The Cards were now even on their West Coast trip.

The winning streak reached four the next day . . . John Tudor pitched a six-hitter . . . Willie McGee homered . . . The Cards beat San Francisco 4–0.

"We're making the big plays both in the field and on offense," said Jack Clark. "We aren't exactly wearing out the ball but we are getting the hits when we need them."

"I've been impressed by the Cardinals as a team," said San Francisco manager Jim Davenport. "I think they are the best in our league. They have solid starting pitching and their bullpen is almost as good."

The bullpen was prominent when the Cardinals proceeded to San Diego. St. Louis spotted San Diego a 6–0 lead, then rebounded for a 9–6 victory. Kurt Kepshire lasted only 4⅓ innings but Ricky Horton, Ken Dayley, and Jeff Lahti combined to produce the Cardinals' fifth straight triumph. Jack Clark hit his 19th homer, Vince Coleman stole two bases, and Terry Pendleton garnered the game-winning RBI.

"That's the type of game that could make a difference in the season," said Coleman, who also had four hits. "It's definitely one to remember.

Rightfielder Andy Van Slyke began spring training at first base, but was moved to the outfield when Jack Clark took the spot.

Steve Braun has provided consistent bench power, especially on the midseason West Coast trip.

Van Slyke chases down a ball in Wrigley Field as centerfielder Willie McGee backs up the play.

"There's just a great atmosphere here. It seems like everything we're doing right now is good and positive. There's not much more you can ask for."

If San Diego manager Dick Williams could have asked for something, he would have requested his team to hold a 6–0 lead. With the loss, the 1984 National League pennant winners fell 3½ games behind the Dodgers.

"I have no comment to make," Williams said to the writers. "You saw it. You write it."

Here's what happened:

Steve Braun continued his West Coast heroics by leading off the ninth with a double off ace reliever Goose Gossage. He scored on Coleman's single. Coleman stole second, went to third on Willie McGee's groundout and scored when Carmelo Martinez dropped Tom Herr's deep flyball for an error.

One out later, Jack Clark walked and Terry Pendleton lined a single to score Herr. Centerfielder Al Bumbry threw wildly on the play to allow Clark to score and when the ball skipped past catcher Terry Kennedy, Pendleton came all the way around to score.

"It was a bizarre ending for a bizarre game," said Kennedy. "There's no good time for a game like this, except maybe the day after you've clinched the pennant."

The teams managed to play a much tidier ball game the next day, but the result was the same. St. Louis won 2–1 on a 12th-inning RBI by Ozzie Smith. Joaquin Andujar went 11 innings to raise his record to 17–4. Vince Coleman stole his 69th base. Ken Dayley pitched a flawless 12th for his seventh save.

St. Louis's six-game winning streak ended the following day, with Andy Hawkins and Goose Gossage combining for a 2–0 victory. The Cardinals had only five hits. Three thousand miles away, the Mets

Former Giant Jack Clark slides safely into third against his former team. Clark went on to score on an Ozzie Smith single.

swept a double-header from Houston to pull within 2½ games of first place.

St. Louis's one-game losing streak ended the following day, with John Tudor and Jeff Lahti combining on a 4–2 victory. Darrell Porter collected his third game-winning RBI. McGee and Pendleton both went 3 for 4.

The Cardinals left the West Coast having compiled a 7–4 record there. They had survived the guacamole, the palm trees, and the other ball clubs. They led by 3½. They also faced a change in fortunes.

WE INTERRUPT THIS SEASON . . .

A funny thing had happened on the way to the All-Star game. At a July 15 meeting in Chicago, the Major-League Players' Association had set an August 6th strike date. Their decision did little to heighten hilarity in baseball's midsummer party, but it did raise interesting possibilities for the Cardinals.

The 1981 strike had shown that funny things could happen. . . things like split seasons. It made you think. If a strike

Kurt Kepshire thanks Tito Landrum for helping him get the win against the Cubs.

came, and it proved to be a long one, then the regular season might be wiped out and the teams in first place would be declared the division winners. With a 3½-game lead, the Cardinals appeared favorably positioned.

But before the strike could be dealt with, there were still seven games to play. After an off day, the Redbirds came to Wrigley Field for a three-game series. They started well, pounding the Cubs 11–3. Kurt Kepshire went eight strong innings, Willie McGee collected his 11th game-winning RBI, and Vince Coleman stole his 70th base. It was just about the last good thing that happened to the Cardinals before the strike deadline.

On Wednesday, Joaquin Andujar was rocked for five runs in five innings in a 5–2 loss. The Mets beat Montreal and the lead was down to two games. On Thursday, the Cubs pushed across a run in the 14th inning for a 9–8 victory. Larry Bowa laid down a perfect suicide squeeze with one out for the game-winner. The Mets did not play. The lead was down to 1½ games.

Back at Busch Stadium after 14 games on the road, the Cardinals faced Philadelphia for four games. They opened with a 3–2 victory, with John Tudor raising his record to 13–8. The Mets lost to Chicago 2–1. The lead was back up to 2½ games. One Cardinal victory or one New York defeat would put St. Louis in first place on the strike deadline.

On Saturday night, the Phillies beat the Cardinals 6–4 in 10 innings. The game was delayed 44 minutes after the sixth inning, and 57 minutes after the eighth, by rain. It was a problem that would plague the Cardinals all weekend. And they had other problems besides the rain.

Derrel Thomas, a veteran who was unwanted in the off-season, launched a pinch-hit, two-out, two-run double in the 10th to lead the Phillies.

"I knew I could still play," said Thomas. "It was just a matter of who I would play with."

With one out in the 10th, Glenn Wilson and Ozzie Virgil singled off Jeff Lahti.

After Rick Schu flied out, Thomas doubled to left center, scoring both runners easily.

"Last time, Lahti jammed me and I made a note of that," said Thomas. "I wasn't thinking about there being two outs or the score tied in the tenth inning. I was just looking for a ball I could drive."

The Mets beat Chicago 5–4 in 10 innings. The lead was down to 1½ games.

On Sunday, things grew more unpleasant. Kevin Gross fired a four-hitter at the Redbirds, beating them 6–0.

With the bases loaded and none out in the third inning of a scoreless game, Gross faced the Redbirds' third, fourth, and fifth hitters.

Payback can be tough: Clark was hot against the Giants, but catcher Bob Brenly tags him out at the plate on a double-steal attempt. Andy Van Slyke was safe at second.

Joaquin Andujar notched his 20th win in mid-August against Atlanta. Met Dwight Gooden won his 20th on the same day.

"The game could have changed right there," Gross said.

It didn't.

He got Tom Herr to ground into a first-to-home force play. He then struck out Jack Clark and got Darrell Porter on a pop up.

Gross and Joaquin Andujar dueled until a 25-minute rain delay at the end of the seventh inning. The Phillies dropped Andujar to 17–6 by sending 11 men to the plate in a six-run eighth. A two-run double by Ozzie Virgil and run-scoring doubles by Von Hayes and Juan Samuel did little to help Andujar.

"He tightened up," Whitey Herzog said of Andujar. "You never really know after a delay how a pitcher will come out and do."

The Mets beat Chicago 4–1. The lead was a half-game.

Jack Clark plows into Dodger catcher Mike Scioscia at the plate in Los Angeles. Clark was out, but so was Scioscia, knocked unconscious for several minutes.

Monday, August 5, represented the Cardinals' last chance to help themselves land in first place by the strike deadline. They sent Danny Cox against Philadelphia left-hander Shane Rawley. Ouch! The Phillies won it 9–1. The Cardinals collected only five hits. Cox lasted only three innings.

"He's trying to throw everything hard," Herzog said. "They were really hitting him. I thought I was going to have to relieve [centerfielder] Willie [McGee] in the third inning. He [Cox] couldn't get the ball down. He couldn't make any pitches."

The Phillies had floundered for much of the year, but they picked a bad time to show improvement. Rawley and John Russell decided to assemble their game just before the strike.

Rawley pitched his second complete game of the season and Russell clubbed a home run and a double. He had entered the game hitting .230.

"They came in here and kicked the heck out of us," said Herzog. "They won three but they should have won them all."

It was a brutal commentary by Herzog.

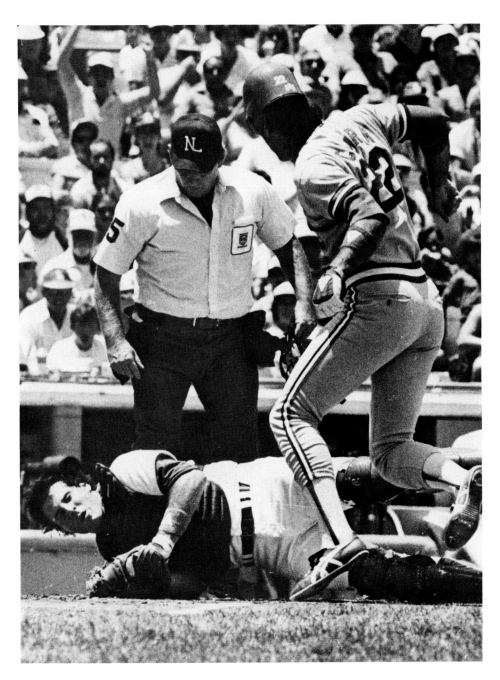

Not only that, but the other news of the day was bad, too. The negotiators reported no progress in avoiding a strike. Worse than that, the Mets pounded the Cubs 7–2. Darryl Strawberry hit three home runs. The Mets led the division by a half-game.

So this was where the Cardinals found themselves. They had survived a poor start. They had assembled a bullpen. They had avoided disaster on the West Coast. They were receiving great seasons from Tom Herr, Willie McGee, and Jack Clark. In Joaquin Andujar, Danny Cox, and John Tudor, they boasted three excellent starters. Vince Coleman was running, and Ozzie Smith was solid at short.

Yet, given a chance to wrap up the division, faced with a situation where they could help themselves, the Cardinals had responded poorly. If the season had ended on August 5, St. Louis would have finished in second place.

7
BORN TO RUN

Willie McGee began the 1982 season in Louisville, Kentucky. By October, he was bouncing off the left center-field wall in County Stadium, Milwaukee, in the World Series. It was a jump that Cardinal fans measured not with an odometer but with a seismograph. McGee's quick rise during that rookie season foreshadowed the rapid progress he would later make to become one of baseball's most competent—if overlooked—players.

Born on November 2, 1958, in the San Francisco area, McGee came to the Cardinals in one of the more lopsided trades ever made by Whitey Herzog. On October 21, 1981, the Cards sent pitcher Bob Sykes to the Yankees for McGee. He was not a big name, even though he had just hit .322 with 7 homers and 63 RBI for the Yanks' farm club in Nashville. He was lost in a Yankee farm system at a time when the major-league club was enjoying success with veterans.

Sykes quietly faded from baseball. McGee did not. In Louisville, he hit .291 in 13 games before being called up to the Cardinals because of an injury to David Green. The Cardinals showed no reluctance to use him, the same way they would later show no problem with placing Vince Coleman in their lineup.

McGee became the regular center-fielder, led all National League rookies with a .296 average, hit .308 with 5 RBI in the National League playoffs, and suddenly found himself in County Stadium during the World Series.

"I can't believe I'm here," he said after Game 3. "But baseball is baseball and anything is possible at any time."

McGee was right, but what he had accomplished a few moments before was slightly improbable. He had dominated a World Series game the way only a few had ever done it: he leaped against the wall in left-center to rob Paul Molitor. He hit two homers, a three-run shot against Pete Vuckovich in the fifth inning and a solo drive in the seventh. In the ninth, he raced to the wall and robbed Gorman Thomas of an extra base hit, maybe a homer.

After the game, someone asked McGee

Willie McGee came to the Cards in one of Herzog's more lopsided trades: pitcher Bob Sykes went to the Yankees in exchange for minor-leaguer McGee. Sykes faded from baseball—McGee did not.

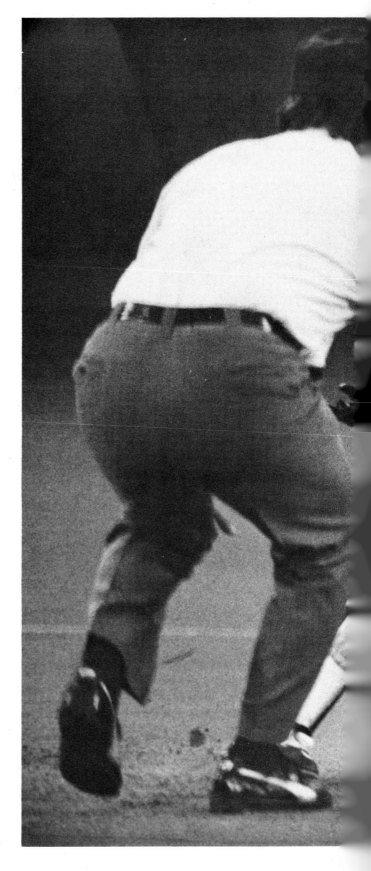

when he had ever hit two home runs in a game.

"Little League," he said.

"If someone had come up to me before the game and offered me 1,000-to-one odds that McGee would hit two homers and specified that they were inside-the-park homers, I would have taken the bet," said Vuckovich. Of the four homers McGee hit during the season, only three went out of the park.

Attention then went to the trade that had brought him to the Cardinals. The irony was clear. Yankee owner George Steinbrenner always wanted his players to reach the World Series. Now, one of them had.

"I would like to thank him for giving me the chance to play professional baseball," McGee said. "And I would like to thank

McGee is safe at second as Philly Juan Samuel misses with the tag.

Ozzie is always a sure bet in the field, but his hitting ha
been consistent as well in 198

The only time McGee doesn't speed around the bases is when he hits a home run—like this three-run blast off Giant pitcher Mark Davis.

Willie races back to the bag before Met Keith Hernandez can pick him off first base. Of course, the biggest race of all was the one that developed between their two teams in the NL East.

him for giving me the chance to play in a fine organization that has four coaches on every level. He prepared me well for this situation."

One of six children and the son of a Deacon of the Pentecostal Church, McGee was the Yankee number 1 choice in the secondary phase of the January 1977 free-agent draft. He spent five seasons in the Yankee chain.

"I had never seen Willie McGee play before we got him," said Herzog. "We had three or four scouting reports on him."

Now, the entire baseball community had a scouting report on McGee. He threw right, and batted from both sides of the plate. He ran like crazy. He was born to run, and Herzog stuck him in center and left him there.

In McGee's second year in the majors, he hit .286 with 39 stolen bases. He made the All-Star team and won a Gold Glove. At one point, he was successful on 17 straight steal attempts. He hit only five home runs, one inside the park, but he drove in 75 runs.

SENSATIONAL!

By 1984, McGee had become one of the premier Cardinals. He led the club in average, at-bats, runs, hits, and triples. It represented superb stature for a player who had been stuck in the Yankee farm system and responded with simple wisdom.

"A lot of us were in the same boat," he said. "You just have to keep rowing."

Despite his accomplishments, McGee did not peak in the majors until the 1985 season. The year began slowly, with McGee on the bench nursing minor hurts. He pinch hit a single on Opening Day, and finally made a start in the third game of the season, going 1 for 5. He missed some more games. Then things began to happen.

On May 6, he went 4 for 4, and picked up his second game-winning RBI. . . . On May 15, he helped beat the Padres. . . . By the end of July, he owned 11 game-winners. . . . He went 5 for 6 to raise his league-leading average to .345 on July 30.

Not exactly poetry, but it works—most of the time. Unfortunately, this ball got past McGee for a triple by the Phillies' Rick Schu.

In an August 10 doubleheader in Philadelphia, he showed the Phillies something they are unlikely to forget. He collected seven hits, three in the first game and four in the second. In the nightcap, he produced his 13th game-winning RBI.

Less than a week later, McGee delivered another extraordinary doubleheader, going 3 for 4 in the opener and 2 for 3 in the nightcap as the Cards swept the Pirates to remain close to first-place New York.

By August 22, he had his average up to .361, one of the highest season averages ever delivered by a switch hitter. He had also established credentials for another key award—the MVP. With the Cardinals in contention, he became a possibility. Tom Herr, Vince Coleman, Jack Clark, and Joaquin Andujar all had some credentials, but McGee was the man. If they won.

No matter what happened, the Cardinals might have laughed to recall a moment in 1982 when McGee was a candidate to be returned to the minors. Gene Tenace had come off the disabled list and someone had to go to make room.

"I don't know what would have happened if Willie had been strictly a right-handed hitter," former Card executive Joe McDonald said at that time. "It's always a great advantage when you can switch hit. That, and he was hot."

In 1985, he was even hotter.

8
THAT'S A WINNER

Essentially, every major leaguer is born to run. The lure of the pennant chase must grab him. Baseball played in the crisp of October is the goal. If not, then something is wrong. The player doesn't belong.

Much less certain, however, is the way to October. The team that wins the most games winds up there, but how to win? Every baseball fan knows some of the answers.

Good starting pitching helps. The kind that Joaquin Andujar, John Tudor, and Danny Cox provide. Then comes defense up the middle. Anybody want to talk about Ozzie Smith? The Golden Year helps, too. Willie McGee's .361 average falls into this category. A bullpen doesn't hurt, either. Jeff Lahti, Ken Dayley, and Ricky Horton did their job. The bench, with Steve Braun and Tom Nieto and Tito Landrum, did the same. Then there's manager Whitey Herzog, applying knowledge of the game, and making it work.

A winning chemistry, however, involves more than just these elements. It involves a group of players deciding that they can

win, that they enjoy winning, and enjoy winning together. They look at the stretch run, and decide to seize it.

Even the term "stretch" represents a problem, though. When does it begin? After the All-Star break? In the dog days of August? On Labor Day weekend? Or perhaps when the players assemble the streak that makes them believe in one another?

For the 1985 Cardinals, the stretch began on August 20. They were a half-game out of first place, but were coming off two extra-inning home losses to the Montreal Expos. Also, they were facing a nine-game road trip taking them to Houston, Atlanta, and Cincinnati. If they fared well on the trip, they would be close entering September, with the New York Mets facing one of those harrowing trips to the West Coast.

On August 20, the Card stretch run began poorly. They went to Houston and got blasted 17–2, stretching their losing steak to three.

They were behind 1–0 in the first inning, 3–0 in the second, 9–0 in the third, 11–0 in the fourth, and 12–0 in the fifth. When they

had the audacity to score two runs in the sixth, the Astros took offense and scored five times in the bottom of the inning. The Mets beat San Francisco 3–0, and took a 1½ game lead.

"These kinds of games aren't as hard to swallow as the one-run losses are," said Jack Clark. "They blew us out early, and we were never in the game."

The question was how well the club would respond. After all, resiliency is part of the winning chemistry, also. The Astrodome had buried many teams in the past. Would it now bury the 1985 Cardinals as well?

Not so fast, gravedigger. Thanks to a pinch-hit, three-run homer by Darrell Porter in the ninth, the Cards beat Houston 7–4 to move back within a half-game of the lead.

"We really haven't been playing very well fundamentally," said Herzog. "I don't know what's wrong. I sure didn't want to lose four in a row."

With the score tied 4–4, Porter ripped a Dave Smith fastball over the right-field fence for a three-run homer to provide the victory. It was Porter's seventh home run of the season and his fifteenth RBI in 11 games.

"Obviously, it's very important that we win," said Porter. "September is when it really gets going and there's still a lot of time left."

The next night, the Cardinals went out and won a ball game—when there wasn't much time left.

For eight innings, Houston starter Joe Niekro's knuckleball stifled the Cardinals. He had retired 13 in a row, struck out seven, and had allowed just four hits through the first eight innings.

But with the Astros holding a one-run lead, he knew if St. Louis's Tom Herr got on base to start the ninth, he would be through for the evening. Herr did get on board and Niekro was lifted. Before the inning was over the Cardinals scored twice for a 2–1 victory.

Brian Harper (above, left), **Mike Jorgensen** (above, right), **Tito Landrum** (below, left), **and Mike Lawless** (below, right), **supplied solid support from the bench.**

His bat still in the air, leadoff man Coleman hits the dirt dodging Brave pitcher Rick Mahler's inside fastball.

"It was predetermined," Niekro said. "[Jack] Clark is such a good knuckleball hitter, we felt [reliever Dave] Smith had a better shot at getting him out with his forkball."

Smith did his job, striking out Clark, then gave way to Jeff Calhoun to face the Cardinal left-handed hitters. The plan backfired.

Calhoun, the eventual loser, 1–2, balked Herr to second and walked Tito Landrum before giving up an RBI-single to Brian Harper that tied the game 1–1.

Calhoun then gave up a single to Terry Pendleton that loaded the bases and Bill Dawley relieved.

Dawley got Ozzie Smith to force Landrum at home on a grounder, but with the bases still loaded he walked Mike Jorgensen to force in Harper with the winning run.

"We didn't give them many opportunities, but they took advantage of the one break we gave them," said Houston manager Bob Lillis. "That's one of the reasons why they're as high up in the standings as they are."

The victory enabled St. Louis to stay a half-game behind the Mets, who held first place by blanking the San Francisco Giants 7–0.

"We prefer easy ones," Jorgensen said. "We've come back and done it [won] a few times. We had a break to start the [ninth] inning. We just go out there every day and play to win."

Ricky Horton, 2–2, picked up the win, pitching the eighth inning in relief of John Tudor. Ken Dayley pitched the ninth to earn his 10th save.

Having won two of three in Houston, the Cards moved on to Atlanta. Joaquin Andujar opened the series by reaching the 20-victory plateau. Andy Van Slyke hit a two-run homer in a 6–2 victory.

Andujar, 20–7, became the first National League pitcher to win 20 games in consecutive years since Houston's Joe Niekro won 21 games in 1979 and 20 in 1980. Andujar became the first Cardinal 20-game winner in two straight years since Hall of Famer Bob Gibson won 20 in 1969 and 23 in 1970.

That is how the Cardinals entered the stretch. They still faced many foes. A trip to New York awaited them, and they would later entertain the Mets at Busch Stadium.

By the end of August, they were in first place, staring at a long September. But one thing was sure—the Cards were born to run. And they were running.

APPENDIX
ST. LOUIS CARDINALS
1985 ROSTER

MANAGER   Whitey Herzog (24)
COACHES   Hal Lanier (8), Nick Leyva (16),
          Dave Ricketts (3), Mike Roarke
          (4), Red Schoendienst (2)

PITCHERS

No.	Name
47	Andujar, Joaquin
36	Boever, Joe
39	Campbell, Bill
34	Cox, Danny
46	Dayley, Ken
31	Forsch, Bob
49	Horton, Rick
50	Kepshire, Kurt
32	Lahti, Jeff
30	Tudor, John

CATCHERS

No.	Name
23	Nieto, Tom
15	Porter, Darrell

INFIELDERS

No.	Name
22	Clark, Jack
11	DeJesus, Ivan
28	Herr, Tom
19	Jorgensen, Mike
12	Lawless, Tom
9	Pendleton, Terry
1	Smith, Ozzie

OUTFIELDERS

No.	Name
26	Braun, Steve
29	Coleman, Vince
25	Harper, Brian
21	Landrum, Tito
51	McGee, Willie
18	Van Slyke, Andy

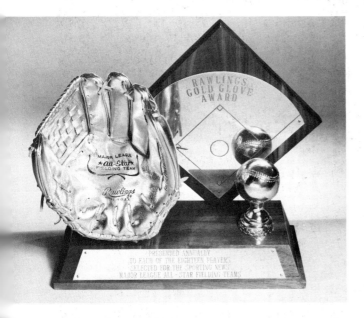